$2/00

E
PICTURE
BOOK
MIL

MARGARET MILLER

BiG
AND
LiTTLE

GREENWILLOW BOOKS NEW YORK

Big foot, little foot.
Room to grow.

Big hand, little hand.
Hold on tight.

Big dog, little dog.
Off we go.

Big hat, little hat.
All dressed up.

Big truck, little truck.
Fun to ride.

Big girl, little girl.
Play with me.

Big ball, little ball.
Upside down.

Big fruit, little fruit.
Good to eat.

Big block, little block.
Build a house.

Big boy, little boy.
Read to me.

Big box, little box. What's inside?

For my **BiG** sister, Anny,

and my **LiTTLE** brother, Mike

My special thanks to all the people—big and little—who appear in this book:
Dave and Colin Kirkpatrick; Janice and Jillian Williams; Michael Olbermann;
Samantha Romano; Kevin Coomaraswamy; Sophie and Serena Silverberg;
Elaine, Caroline, and Sumner Richter; Evan Solomon; Eve Teitelbaum;
Brian Moore and Christopher VanHouten; and Taylor Moore.

The full-color photographs were reproduced from 35-mm Kodachrome slides.
The text type is Futura Light.
Copyright © 1998 by Margaret Miller
All rights reserved. No part of this book may be reproduced
or utilized in any form or by any means, electronic or mechanical, including photocopying,
recording, or by any information storage and retrieval system, without permission in writing
from the Publisher, Greenwillow Books, a division of William Morrow & Company, Inc.,
1350 Avenue of the Americas, New York, NY 10019.
http://www.williammorrow.com
Printed in Singapore by Tien Wah Press
First Edition   10 9 8 7 6 5 4 3 2 1

Library of Congress Cataloging-in-Publication Data

Miller, Margaret, (date) 1945
Big and little / by Margaret Miller.
   unp.   em. ill
Summary: Photographs and easy text introduce the concepts of size and opposites.
   ISBN 0-688-14748-8 (trade).   ISBN 0-688-14749-6 (lib. bdg.)
1. Size perception—Juvenile literature.   2. Size judgment—Juvenile literature.
[1. Size.]   I. Title.   BF299.S5M55   1998   153.7'52—dc21   97-17242   CIP   AC